My Thoughts

as a Black Man

JB Lee

I AM Publications

My Thoughts as a Black Man

I AM Publications

(617) 564-1060

contact@iampubs.com

www.iampubs.com

ISBN: 978-1-943382-31-6

Table of Contents

Dedication

This book is dedicated to my mother and father. Without your love and

support, I don't know where I would be.

Introduction

First of all, I would like to say thank you. For your love and support on the creation of this book. *My Thoughts as a Black Man* is my introspective experiences over the past decade of my life. I was going to keep these to myself and never share these poems and essays I wrote but due to people being in my life and filling my heart with courage I decided to make these writings public. Inside of this book, I hope to take your mind on a visual journey like I do with my artwork. It's like a word painting; where thoughts are colors and the paper becomes my canvas. Some of these thoughts may not be for everyone due to today's climate regarding religion, politics, and culture. Nonetheless, this is art. And the power of art is to strike a nerve. Whether striking that nerve is for the greater good or not is a matter of opinion that, frankly, I am not concerned with. I did this for me. First, to get over a fear of my growth. Second, to show my family that Jamil is even more than what I knew I could be. Most importantly, I did this for God—to, again, get over my fear. In closing, I hope to take you to a higher place of hope, love, and existence with this book. I hope you love reading it just as much as I've

enjoyed writing it over the past ten years. And, always, thank you for

your love and support in my creative journey.

Forward

Jamil. This is your first book, and I know everything that you're going through right now. There's a lot of excitement and nervousness for all the right reasons. Oh, I just forgot about this as well. This is a poetry book. I love the fact that this is something you wanted to achieve and thank God for the fact that it's happening. When I wrote my first book, it didn't scratch the surface of what I wanted to accomplish, so don't stop at one book.

What are your thoughts as a Black Man? I know my thoughts as one but what are yours? I'm glad we're going to find out what that is. I'm glad you are using your voice to share your thoughts as we need newer voices to shed light on every aspect of being black and being black men in this day and age. It's time for us to be the light carriers. It's time for us to show the world who we truly are. It's time not to only give our thoughts but time to show through actions. We as a people always showed through the written works how we were able to really show the world who we truly are. From great black thinkers, poets, rappers, etc. Let's blaze this new path and show what we can achieve.

Jamil, AKA Mill, I'm very proud of you and the work that you've done to show the beauty, love, hurt, thoughts, strength, of what it's like to be black. Now you're giving your thoughts as a black man. Let us not be afraid of what the world may say, and let us be focused on what God has put in our hearts.

Love You,

Kelvin "LoFi Kelvy" Wilson

Section 1:

Love and Relationships

Will You

Will you just connect with me...

Will you just love me...

Will you just lay with me...

Will you just be...

Will you just hold on to me...

Will you just... will you just...

Anxiety

I can't breathe —

but I'm still breathing.

Every inhale feels like an argument,

and my lungs keep losing.

My heart don't knock politely anymore —

it kicks.

Every time I try to rest,

it starts running,

dragging me behind it like a ghost

who forgot how to stop haunting.

I tell people I'm fine

so they don't worry.

But "fine" is just a code word

for "fighting invisible things

in public places."

Anxiety don't ask permission —

it just moves in,

starts rearranging furniture in my mind,

leaves the lights on at 3 a.m.

and whispers,

"You forgot something again."

My mother says pray.

My therapist says breathe.

But nobody says what to do

when the prayers sound like static

and the breathing feels like drowning.

So, I write.

I write to keep the panic

from becoming prophecy.

To keep the noise

from learning my name.

Euphoria

My job is to tell you a story...

One about love, one about struggle...

A story about a man and a woman...

A story about heart, a story about us...

My love song, my view of Black love...

The touch. The sight. The kiss. The hugs...

You, me, us, eternity.

Will you be my euphoria?

Brand New

Fresh kicks

opened on a Saturday night —

brand new is how I feel.

Crisp polo,

new jeans,

fit just right —

brand new is how I feel.

Bottle of my favorite cologne —

brand new is how I feel.

You by my side forever —

brand new is how I feel.

Newports

First time I let you touch my lips —

I was hooked.

The taste tingled —

not just my lips,

but the inner core

of who I was.

You're hard to let go.

Addictive.

I'm submissive

to your want for me —

I need you.

I need you

like crack needs dealers,

like Christians need believers,

like pimps need hoes.

You're the first thing I wake up to,

the last thing I go to bed with.

My best friend

and my worst enemy.

I need to give you up —

but I can't.

If I could, I would.

But I can't.

You're like Newports —

my addiction.

The Ave

Waiting on the corner —

it's bitter cold.

Wind hits my chest,

cuts through my soul.

I can't take no more,

but just before I walk away —

here come my customer.

5'9", lips of gold,

a body carved by rhythm.

Every step she takes

brings her one closer to heaven —

mine.

She comes to me,

eyes bright,

mouth ready to ask one question —

but I open my hand first.

She takes it —

and with it,

my heart.

I do.

Give you the world and everything in it.

I do.

Give you my hopes,

my dreams,

my innermost thoughts.

I met her on the Ave.

Relate to You

You know what—

I can relate to you.

I can understand how you feel,

because we are connected.

Connected on the same path,

going in the same direction,

at the same time—

headed to the same place.

But can I ask you something?

Because I don't just want to follow you.

I want to lead with you.

Understand you.

Grow with you.

Become your everything.

So here's my question:

Are you ready?

...Where are we going?

Just Us

Me and you—

against all odds,

we gonna shine.

What's mine is yours,

and what's mine… is still ours.

Together we gonna rule—

not just a block,

but the world.

Don't stop.

Don't stop.

Until the day I take my last breath,

I'm gonna hold you up.

Never give up.

We enough—

for each other,

for one another.

I know you still down.

And if you don't know,

just know this one thing—

It's just us.

Uncommon

It's not uncommon

for me to come to you this way.

My heart,

my soul,

my desires—

I lay them down in front of you.

You are my peace.

From you, I get my joy.

You fill all voids.

But still—

I struggle.

I struggle with being alone.

Not having someone

to share this life with.

No hand to hold.

No simple "hello."

No complex "I love you."

It hurts me.

It derails me.

Am I not worthy of loving someone?

Am I not worthy of beauty in my life?

Am I not worthy of caring for my reflection

with attention?

Please—send her to me.

So I can tell her I love her.

So I can reflect your love back to her.

Please tell her I love her.

And only you will be above her.

Please tell her...

I love her.

This is not uncommon.

Queen

You—

you are so much more than what you see.

You are the quality portion of me.

You are my heart,

my vision,

the piece of me I can't live without.

I thank God for you—

you're right for me, no doubt.

I will honor you,

respect you,

and be all up in my feelings for you.

You are my queen.

The poem that crowns love as divine

—before you realize how much it costs to carry it.

Taken

My heart is empty.

My feelings are cold.

Subjected to old memories,

disillusioned by illusions of grandeur.

My impressions are lost inside feelings

that run deep as the Nile.

I can't keep denying my emotions.

My heart runs wild.

My thoughts outweigh my heart,

and my heart outweighs my mind.

My mind is tied to my soul—

and my soul is losing this battle.

I can't keep thinking about you.

Can't keep wanting you

and pretending that it's okay.

You're already...

taken.

90's Love

See, I want that 90s sitcom kind of love—

That Martin and Gina kind of love,

That love that's dope,

That love that's truth,

That love that's not afraid to be vulnerable.

I want that 90s sitcom kind of love—

That Dewayne and Whitley kind of love,

That love that's giving, forgiving,

That don't quit kind of love,

The kind of love that makes you see a different world.

I want that 90s sitcom kind of love.

Who's Gonna Love You

Who's gonna love you the way I do?

Be there for you,

Your shoulder to cry on,

Your ear to listen.

Who's gonna love you the way I do?

Hold you when times get tough,

Wipe your eyes when you've had enough,

Through thick and thin—I'm there.

Who's gonna love you the way I do?

Support your dreams until they come true,

Be your producer, your emotional support.

Places we've never been...

(pause)

Unselfish.

Places We Never Have Been

We are in a place that we have never been—

Closer to our destiny, closer to our sin.

The benefits of you are unlimited within.

You can only give me what I need:

My deepest desire.

It's not in between your legs,

What I want are your thoughts,

Your hopes, your dreams, wrapped up and given to me,

So I can protect them, honor them, respect them.

This is the place where we can build, grow,

And have the success we both desire.

This is the place we've never been—

Unselfish.

Hope That I

You hope that I can be the man you need,

A man of God, a man of integrity,

An honest man.

I just hope that I can be a man—

A man I can be proud of,

A man as real with himself

As he is with you.

Hopefully, I can just be a man...

And the rest will come.

What Do You Want from Me

What do you want from me?

What can I do?

Nothing but love you.

Nothing but love you through your pain.

Nothing but love you through your weakness,

despite how you treat me.

See, when you love somebody — that woman —

you put up with more of her shit.

Some hard nights.

Some yelling fights.

But love heals.

What can I do?

Love you through what you're going through.

I know you. I adore you.

I put up with this shit.

What do you want me to do?

I could leave —

but I'll be back.

Because deep down, you ain't going nowhere.

I know you love me too.

Your words say it.

Your actions, past this hard spot, do the same.

So I'll stay a while longer.

That's what I did.

That's what you wanted me to do.

Her

I can smell her scent — it touches my soul.

She graced my presence with her mind.

Touched me with her body.

And it drove me crazy.

I think I might be in love.

Or at least falling.

I don't want to dive in too deep —

but she tempts me anyway.

Her hair smells like shea butter and roses,

mixed with temptation.

Her skin is as soft as a bed of flowers.

Her eyes are deep —

I can see into her soul, maybe deeper.

I think I've reached her essence.

Lovers

I love her, but I love her too.

In different ways, I love them both.

One nurtures me, encourages me,

and I love to be around her.

But with the other,

I love how she talks (a little dirty),

treats me like a man — but not completely.

And when I get in between her legs after we argue all day —

it's heaven.

Not her (wife).

She's sweet, kind, pleasant.

We don't even fight.

Her body is fire.

She's the mother of my kids, my first love, my best friend.

But I need them both.

They serve different purposes.

One for business, one strictly for pleasure.

I love them both.

Section 2:

Personal Growth and Reflection

Out the Womb (Adolescence)

Out the womb —

adolescence.

Immature.

Maturing.

Evolving.

Stagnant.

Reinventing.

Love.

Reflecting.

Acknowledging.

Knowing when to let go.

Reflection, part two —

picking up the pieces,

reliving the past.

Faith.

Future.

Structure.

The cycle begins again —

not born this time,

but rebuilt.

Mr. Forgettable

They only remember you

when they need something.

That's the curse, ain't it?

To be essential in someone's storm

but invisible in their sunlight.

I've been the backbone,

the late-night call,

the shoulder,

the prayer,

the "you always understand."

And yet somehow,

I'm still the ghost

in their photo albums.

They post quotes about loyalty

but never tag the ones who lived it.

I used to get angry —

but now I just disappear quieter.

There's a peace

in not explaining your absence

to people who never noticed your presence.

They call me "Mr. Forgettable."

But that's a lie.

I remember everything.

I remember every "thank you"

that came without staying.

Every "you're different"

that meant "you won't be chosen."

But it's cool.

I learned the art of fading —

of letting go

before the light does.

Megatron

He just sits there — waiting.

Wondering. Searching.

A forgotten leader,

wanting to be sought —

for knowledge.

But where can that thirst lead?

Down a path of distraction — or grace.

Destruction — or just keeping pace.

We can't honor those who disrespected us,

but we can take —

take that beating that was meant to break us.

Yet we didn't break.

We built.

We created the culture they now live in.

Take it back —

like your culture is precious.

He said, "Stop being weak."

I asked, "How can I be strong when my ship leaks?"

He looked at me,

eyes glowing —

not with light,

but disgust.

Night of 1000 Fists

Are you dying?

No — but inside, I'm trying.

Crying.

Tired of all the pain,

the cover-ups,

the lying.

Is my face bruised? No —

that's just my melanin.

Mistaken for something it's not —

used to cover up your own sin.

I can't win.

But I'm gonna win —

because the mold's been broken.

No longer a token,

I'm focused on more than the notion.

"What you gonna do?"

Fight back?

If I do, I'm dead.

If I don't, I'm dead.

The only way to live — is to dream.

Dream like a king.

But dreaming don't last forever.

If it did —

we'd all eat,

instead of taking beatings.

We'd rise off the floor,

stand from the throne —

not to repeat what was done,

but to be better

than before.

But that's just me —

dreaming.

I Need to Learn

I need to learn how to say things differently.

Instead of saying "off myself,"

I need to say —

"I'm having thoughts."

That should be enough

to trigger what I need.

For you —

it's a good thing to show your art.

It's not a stress

unless you let it become one.

Be who you are.

Be open with her.

Communicate your feelings

and your emotions.

You are guarded.

Time to put that wall down.

Response

I talked to God today.

Told Him all that was on my mind—

how valuable He is to my life.

How I can't move forward without Him.

No response.

I talked to God today.

Told Him He's the Holy of Holies,

my rock,

my need,

my everything.

No response.

I talked to God today—

and told Him,

"I just want to listen."

He responded.

So Much

I've burned one too many bridges,

Built too many walls.

My soul hurts for love—

Will I answer its call?

My heart yearns for you,

Wanting to feel your touch.

My soul needs you,

Needs you so much.

Live and Learn
1 Kings 12

How many of us want the good things—

The wisdom of God on our side,

A following that believes in our dream?

But the answer's right in front of us—

Every day.

We have to learn to take advice

From the people who truly care

About our best interest.

The generation before us

Holds great knowledge—

They've been there before.

Even if they haven't walked our path,

Their wisdom is worth the listen.

Never take counsel

From those with less experience

Than the ones who've survived the fire.

Let wisdom prevail.

Virgil Was My Jordan

When I look back on my life as an artist, I can name a lot of people who shaped the way I see the world. There were family members, like my cousin Warren Parks — one of the greatest artists I've ever known. There were teachers like Ms. Woods, Mr. Bradshaw, and Marc Schumer, who each gave me something different to hold onto.

But when I think about the two people who had the biggest impact on me as a human being, I always land on Michael Jordan and, later in life, Virgil Abloh.

I loved Jordan — not just for the highlights, but for the movement he created, for the intensity that came with every step he took on that court. You could feel his hunger to be great. It wasn't arrogance; it was purpose. It's rare to witness that kind of relentless focus — someone who wants to dominate with their craft every single time they show up.

As I got older and started learning more about another one of my passions — business — I admired Jordan even more. He wasn't just an athlete; he was a brand, a businessman, a symbol of ownership and precision. Watching him taught me that talent could be turned into structure, and passion could become legacy.

Then came Virgil.

I first heard his name in my late twenties or early thirties — I think it was during a Kanye interview. Kanye said something about a guy named Virgil who was behind the scenes, a creative force even he admired. That caught me off guard. Because if Kanye was giving someone else that kind of praise, I had to know who that person was.

So, I started digging. That's when I discovered Pyrex Vision, Virgil's first clothing line — or at least the first one that I knew about. I was drawn to it instantly. I loved how he took something familiar — a household name like Pyrex — and flipped it into something entirely new. That spoke to me. I've always loved taking, turning, and transforming — reshaping the ordinary into something unexpected.

Everything Virgil did felt like art in motion — like watching Jordan pull off a dunk from the free-throw line or hit a fadeaway jumper with three seconds left on the clock. He had that same instinct for greatness, but his court was fashion, design, and culture itself.

And then, just like Jordan hoisting the trophy, I watched Virgil have his championship moment — becoming the first Black artistic director at Louis Vuitton. That moment hit me hard. Not because aligning with a white-owned fashion house is the ultimate victory, but because anytime a Black creative can breach those walls — can change the system from the inside — it's a win for all of us.

Jordan conquered the court.

Virgil conquered the culture.

And for me, Virgil was my Jordan. Watching him showed me that art, business, and legacy could coexist — that the game isn't just about playing; it's about redefining the rules while you're in it.

That's what greatness looks like.

That's what I chase every day.

Section 3:

Social and Cultural Commentary

Delusional

There's a lot to unpack here, so I'm sorry in advance. This might take more of your time than usual.

I'm sick of feeling like I'm delusional.

Delusional, you ask?

Yes—delusional. I'm tired of feeling like when I see racism, it's just a one-time thing. That it's so isolated that I'd be crazy if it happened again.

Do you understand me? How many times, as a Black man in this country, have I been called the N-word—hard R?

How many times have I walked down the street, and someone grabs their purse... or their child?

Bitch, I've got two kids. I don't want yours. I don't want your $2.50, or the stick of gum in your worn-out, fake-ass Gucci purse.

Oh, right... that's delusional, isn't it?

I'm sick of hearing how my culture is fucked up,

but I don't hear anyone talk about their own culture making money off

of it.

I don't hear about anyone else's responsibility for the fucked-up behavior

of our people—the government, not everyday folks.

I definitely don't hear anyone praising Black culture when your favorite

sports player does something you like.

Oh, sorry... I'm still fucking delusional.

And I'm so tired of these fake-ass "race soldiers"

who think because I'm Black, I'm weak.

Again—bitch, do you know my stock?

No, I'm not talking about what's in my pocket. I'm talking about what's

in my heart, my soul.

My stock is from the South. My stock is from hard work. My stock is

from defiance.

My stock is from the Panthers, from the activists.

Nigga, fuck you if you think I'm about to be silent!

You can try to silence me, but that won't stop what's coming… for you in

this life or the next.

Oh, I'm sorry… that's delusional, right?

Shock

We are inside of a state of shock—

Black man, black woman,

Underpaid, overworked, marginalized,

Carrying the pain of 400 years

Of scars that still have not healed.

We are inside of a state of shock—

Stomped on by our own through negative hustling.

Pick your poison:

A needle, a bullet, or a payday loan—

Either way, they gonna kill you,

Internal, external.

Are you ready to fight this battle within?

We are inside a state of shock—

Group economics ain't working for us,

Years of conditioning lead to teachings

That reached our masses

With extreme prejudice.

Now, instead of building, we break each other down—

Crabs in a bucket.

It is an unnatural situation with an unnatural response.

We are inside a state of shock.

They Keep Asking

They keep asking,

"What do you want?"

I want to be treated like a human being.

I want the pain to stop—

the pain from grief,

from mistreatment,

from the scars you can't see.

I want to be treated equal,

to live without looking over my shoulder.

To dream—

and not feel like I can't achieve

because hope got evicted

from my neighborhood.

They keep on asking,

"What do you want?"

I want to stand on my own.

Not depend on another

to live the so-called American dream.

Not feel like crime is my only option.

Not say, "Damn... maybe if I could hoop or rap,

I could make it."

They keep asking.

But what I want—

is simple.

I want to go home.

Like you.

To not feel disconnected,

to not wonder if I'll make it back

to my family.

I'm tired of being disconnected

from a country that doesn't love me,

but expects me to love it back.

I want to matter—

not by your standard,

but on my own.

Stop asking me what I want—

and start working with me.

What Happened

Where has all of our talent gone?

You can always tell when a society — or a culture — is getting ready to crumble. You can see it in two places: its art and its music, and more importantly, in how the people respond to both.

In all my travels — the galleries I've walked through, the shows I've seen, the paintings I've sold — I can tell you clearly: America is folding in on itself. Not because there's no talent, but because talent has been confused with work ethic.

Just because you pick up a brush doesn't mean you're a painter.

Just because you pick up a camera doesn't make you a photographer.

Just because you pick up a microphone doesn't make you the next big thing.

And most importantly — just because you work hard does not entitle you to be an artist.

Art demands something deeper than labor.

It demands calling.

It demands want.

By "want," I mean this: you must want to learn, want to grow, want to evolve — before you can truly create. Too often, I see people without talent but with a strong work ethic getting ahead, not because they're better, but because they've learned how to feed the machine.

But the machine doesn't need more oil.

The machine needs a driver — someone talented enough to steer it toward something real.

Right now, we don't have enough of those. That's why, as a culture, we're failing.

One: Hard work has overtaken talent. I'm not saying you shouldn't work for what you want — you absolutely should. But there are far too many talentless people crowding the lane, diluting the very fabric of artistic humanity.

One: We've lost the want. I meet so many people who call themselves artists just because it sounds good, not because they feel it in their bones. You can't just want to be an artist — art must want you back. If the art doesn't call you, you're not in the right lane. Step aside and let those who are truly called do the work of changing hearts and minds.

Two: Where are our leaders?

Maybe I'm old school, but I thought the purpose of art was to lift others — to help another artist reach the next level. We don't have enough of that anymore. Too many of our so-called leaders are accountants, curators, and middlemen — people who don't create but control, who sit behind desks making decisions for those of us in the trenches.

They're keeping the machine running, but they can't drive it.

And their driving skills? Somewhere between reckless and asleep at the wheel.

If we want to fix this, we have to fix ourselves first. Artists must reclaim the responsibility of building our own environment — not waiting for permission, not relying on institutions that never had our best interests in mind.

We are the light bearers.

It's on us to bring our culture back to the forefront.

Even though my Christian beliefs might contradict this statement, I know that not every artist is a believer — and that's okay. Faith or not, the one thing we all have control over is selfishness. We can end it by choosing to help one another, by deciding that art is not a competition but a conversation.

When we start leading again, we start healing again.

When we lift each other up, the culture rises with us.

That's what happened — and that's what needs to happen again.

The Land of the Free

Are we?

I ask you again — are we, really?

Are we free,

or is "freedom" just a brand name —

a slogan on the side of a building

that never let us in?

If we were free,

we'd care for each other more.

We'd challenge each other to grow,

not hide behind pulpits, paychecks,

and polished masks.

If we were free,

learning wouldn't feel like trespassing.

We could question,

study,

doubt —

without someone calling us ungrateful.

We are not free.

We are still trained to behave.

Still afraid to fight back

because we think we have too much to lose.

But what if losing it all

was the first step to gaining your life back?

Land of the Free?

I think not.

It's Revolutionary

It's revolutionary

for us — Black men, Black women —

to do anything in this world.

To rest.

To smile.

To laugh.

To feel joy —

that's protest in motion.

Can I just be me?

Can I live?

What if I don't want to smile?

What if I'm tired of performing peace

for people who don't protect mine?

What if my joy lives in silence,

in solitude,

in stillness?

Can I live —

without your gaze,

without your suspicion,

without the weight of always proving I belong?

I don't want to be your revolution.

I just want to breathe,

to love,

to wake up in a world

where living isn't an act of defiance.

I just want to live my life.

Embrace Your Story

You have to understand something: you are an instrument of life.

Every note you play — every decision, every mistake, every victory —

contributes to a larger song that God is composing through you.

Ask yourself: What interest am I furthering?

Whose purpose am I serving?

Your experiences matter. Every one of them. The good, the bad, the

broken, the redeemed — all of it is useful in the hands of the

Creator.

I am a chosen instrument of God.

You are too.

1. Connection

His story connects us.

God's kingdom connects us.

Am I truly embracing the community of believers, or am I trying to live

this faith alone?

We were never meant to walk this life solo.

Embrace the people God places in your path — those who challenge you, those who comfort you, and those who call you higher.

Community is the thread that ties the kingdom together.

2. Transformation

When you embrace your story, you point back to God.

Your testimony isn't just for you — it's a mirror that reflects His power to others.

Your experiences are the bridge that reconcile you — and those who hear you — back to God.

You decide what your rock bottom is.

And when you rise from it, you prove that grace still works.

Acts 9:20 says, "Immediately he began to proclaim Jesus in the synagogues, saying, 'He is the Son of God.'"

Telling your story brings Jesus to life.

There is power in transformation.

So ask yourself: Where has God brought me from?

Because when you tell that truth, you're not just testifying — you're

loving.

And telling your story becomes an act of love.

3. Investment

Let's invest in each other's lives.

By our love for one another, the world will know we are disciples.

The church grows when the people of God grow — when wisdom,

virtue, and faith take root.

Wisdom is choosing what's right when you already know what's wrong.

Faith is living with character when no one is watching.

The youth are watching.

They must see our example.

The church will grow when we invest — not just in buildings, but in

people.

Our chapter in God's story is still being written.

And what we write next depends on how we love.

4. Liberation

Impact your community.

Be vulnerable.

Because freedom begins where the truth is told.

Embrace your story.

Liberation comes from it.

Dangerous in the Mind

The most dangerous place I can be

is inside the mind of someone who never knew me.

Someone who looks at my skin and sees a story they already wrote —

"thug," they say —

and none of my life fits into that box.

Doesn't matter what I've done,

how I hustle,

how I love,

how I father,

how I pray.

All they see is the color and the stereotype heaped on top.

To them, I represent what they fear —

resilience that refuses to be small,

hope that's louder than their excuses,

truth that punctures their comfortable lies.

If they took time — just a minute —

they'd see: I am a father.

A Christian.

An artist.

An entrepreneur.

A lover.

A galvanizer.

A truth seeker.

A friend.

A brother.

An uncle.

But before all that — I'm black —

and to them that equals "thug."

So here I am — dangerous in your mind.

Because what I am breaks your story.

And you don't like stories that don't end like yours.

Palestine

I feel your grief from thousands of miles away.

The loss of life — unbearable.

Generations taken by hate — too much to bear.

I cry.

I'm uneasy.

Restless as a father screams over a lost family,

a wife mourning her husband,

a child left without nurture.

I cry.

I can't side with those who commit atrocities.

I stand with the oppressed.

I stand with the rising spirit.

I stand on the side of right,

even when others think I am wrong.

I understand history.

I understand my moral code.

I understand what I need to do.

But I still cry for you.

Children

Children of God

killing children of God —

expecting heaven as reward

for murder done in His name.

"Thou shall not kill,"

but we do.

Because war pays.

Because hate is currency.

We cannot heal

when our trauma is tradition.

We cannot grow

when our pain is policy.

A twelve-year-old holds a gun,

thinking manhood

is measured in fear.

If God is love —

then where is the love in you?

If you don't give,

you can't live.

And if you can't live,

you're already in the prison

of your soul.

Hell is eternal —

born of your own tongue.

So stop acting like a child.

And grow

the fuck

up.

Stars

What if we been traveling the stars

for thousands of years —

long before rockets,

before fear,

before fences.

Afraid now

to travel past our own backyards.

We been the ones discovering —

not new lands,

but new planets to call home.

And now —

we think a jail cell is a throne.

What if we were second to the Creator,

not made to labor for others,

but to cultivate the mind

to new heights?

Now we're caught up —

timid,

scrolling,

searching for that next high.

What if we were

the astronomers,

the astronauts,

the philosophers —

meant to lead?

But somewhere

we got tricked —

by ego,

by greed,

by acts not humble,

by hearts not human.

What if we were the stars?

Unleashing Creativity on the Black Community for Social Change

Artists are often asked how we can create social change in our own communities. The answer, to me, is simple: do what you think you can't do.

The greatest act of social change an artist can make begins with conquering the word can't. Not just to prove something to the world, but to prove something to yourself — that freedom lives on the other side of fear. Inside every artist, no matter the discipline, lies that one creative risk that makes them dangerous. That risk — the one thing you're most afraid of doing — is where your transformation begins.

Looking back over my twenty-five years as an artist, there was rarely a moment when I let fear decide for me. I dipped my hands in paint and went after what I knew — or thought I knew. I learned photography, mastered streetwear, built hand-drawn graphics, and even learned how to run and operate businesses in music, fashion, and art.

When we launched The International African American Art Museum of Kansas City (IAAAMKC), I didn't have a blueprint. I just knew what needed to be done — and I did it. Today, I'm in the midst of

building something that I believe is special, something that will leave a

mark on Kansas City, and, God willing, ripple across the nation and the

world.

Now, you might be thinking — Jamil, surely something scared

you along the way.

You'd be right. Two things have always scared me as an artist:

disappointing myself, and not giving enough of myself back to my

That's why my latest show, Comics, Cowboys, and Kung Fu, was

one of the most terrifying projects I've ever done. It was a deep dive into

my own childhood — one filled with joy, laughter, and imagination. But

it was also a childhood where, despite all that wonder, I never saw myself

represented. Not in the cartoons I loved, not in the books I read, not

even in the toys I played with.

So when I began painting these memories, I wasn't just creating

art — I was confronting absence. I was painting myself into the story

that had left me out. And when the time came to show the work, I was terrified. What if people didn't understand it? What if they only wanted the version of me they were used to — the familiar, safe Jamil?

But fear has a strange way of revealing purpose. Through that fear, I realized that the work wasn't just for me — it was for us. It was a chance to unleash creativity on the Black community. To show that representation isn't permission; it's reclamation. That to be free, we must heal ourselves, grow ourselves, and remain true to who we are — even when it scares us.

Art is not just what we make — it's what we give. It's how we change hearts, minds, and souls. As artists, we are not just creators; we are galvanizers of culture. We are called to a higher standard. We live art, breathe art, and embody the possibility that others haven't yet imagined.

So if we truly believe that, then we must also believe this:

We are the change we've been waiting for.

We are our own proof — living, breathing testimony that creativity can move nations and heal communities.

We need each other. We need the courage to believe in what we haven't yet seen. And most of all — we need to do the thing we don't believe we can do.

Because when we do, that's when the world changes.

Section 4:

Faith and Spirituality

Jeremiah 29:11

"For I know the plans I have for you," says the Lord.

"Plans to give you hope,

And a future.

Plans to prosper you."

I made that scripture my mantra—

Because God knows the plan for my life.

He won't harm me;

He wants me to prosper—

More faith,

More hope,

More love.

No matter what comes next,

My life is for the glory of God.

He gets the glory

From every direction my life takes.

Because He's had the blueprint

Since before I took my first breath.

Ask yourself:

1. Are you willing to follow, not lead?

2. Are you willing to stay in the fire, and still trust that God wants
   to prosper you?

3. Even when you can't see the future—can you trust that He does?

Notes on Holiness

The first step of holiness—

Is knowing who you are.

Accept your sin.

Then create steps

To step away from it.

Seek wisdom.

Understand—

You are called to be apart from others.

You are called to be holy,

Because you are in direct fellowship

With God and Christ.

Be holy,

Because God is holy.

A holy nation.

A royal priesthood.

Set apart.

When you grow complacent,

When you lose your edge,

You commit spiritual suicide.

(pause, let "spiritual suicide" sit heavy in the air)

Isaiah 6:7 says—

God is like a burning coal.

He's ready to set us apart,

Ready to make our words hot with truth.

Ready to send us out—

Across towns, cities,

Even nations.

He'll blot out our sins

Like they never happened.

But first—

We must come to Him.

We must be willing.

We must be ready.

Are you ready... to be holy?

(deliver "Are you ready" directly to the audience — eye contact)

Inside the holiness of Christ,

Remember this:

Being set apart

Also calls for righteous behavior.

Christ was sinless,

Set apart to die for the sinner—

Us.

The death of Christ

Wasn't just the right thing to do;

It was wisdom in action.

Through His sacrifice,

We can stand righteous before the Father.

Through the cross,

We are made holy.

So flee to the Rock of your salvation.

Run to God,

For He is your refuge.

Salvation and Righteousness
1 Timothy 1:15

Christ came into this world to save sinners—

Of which I am the worst.

He saved me.

I'm reminded daily—

That His righteousness

Is what redeemed me.

Romans 6:6–7 says:

Our old self was crucified with Him,

So that the body of sin

Might be rendered powerless.

Anyone who has died

Has been freed from sin.

Romans 6:12 adds—

Do not let sin reign

In your mortal body.

Holiness is a gift,

But it's one we must work at.

We pursue holiness

Because truth demands it.

We died to sin—

So how can we live in it any longer?

Baptism reminds us—

We died to sin

So we could rise to purpose.

No, that doesn't mean sin can't touch us.

It means we now have a goal:

To strive toward holiness.

Focus

Focus.

Yeah, I struggle with that too.

I know—hard to believe.

An artist, an entrepreneur—

Losing focus?

But I do.

I struggle to stay on my path.

With my art.

With my faith.

With my purpose.

This one's for me,

And for you, Lauren.

Keep your focus.

Keep your heart on God.

The Bible is our focal point—

Our compass.

The closer we get to Him,

The clearer the vision becomes.

Colossians 3:2 says:

"Set your minds on things above,

Not on earthly things."

It's simple but powerful.

Keep your mind on Christ,

Not on "me."

Not my life, my wants, my desires.

When all the attention's on us,

We lose sight of Him.

So—

1. What is your heart set on?

2. What's your mindset when you read this—God or me?

3. Where do you want your focus to be?

Seek First

Matthew 6:33 says:

"Seek ye first the Kingdom,

And all these things will be added unto you."

Seek the rule of God.

Seek His way first.

Yes, it's hard sometimes.

We make mistakes.

We sin.

We're human.

But when we put God first—

Even in the fire—

Everything we need

Will be added to our lives.

Ask yourself:

1.   Are you seeking the Kingdom?

2. What do you want added to your life?

Do It with All Your Might
Ecclesiastes 9:10

"Whatever your hand finds to do,

Do it with all your might."

Because in the realm of the dead,

There's no work,

No plan,

No wisdom.

Whatever your gift is—

Do it.

Whatever God placed in your heart—

Do it with authority.

Live with no regrets.

You get one shot—

Make it great.

With God, with family,

With love, with laughter.

Make it count.

1. What has God put on your heart to do?

2. Are you living your life with no regrets?

Suffer for Good

1 Peter 3:17 says:

"It's better to suffer for doing good,

Than for doing evil."

So ask yourself—

Would you rather suffer now for Christ,

Or later for the world?

I choose to suffer for God.

1. Are you willing to suffer for Christ?

2. What does doing good for Christ mean to you?

Remain Humble

Stay humble.

Humility is the doorway

Through which your gifts will walk.

Remain humble before God—

And you'll start to look more like David.

More like Christ.

You'll be after His heart,

Until one day—

You'll see through His eyes.

Because through humility,

We learn that:

- God causes and expects humility.

- Positive results come from being humble.

And when you kneel low enough,

You rise high enough

To touch Heaven.

(close softly — humble tone, slow breath at the end)

Jesus You're Taking Too Long

Jesus... you're taking too long.

Sometimes God wants you in long-suffering...

The power... the patience... the weight of long-suffering...

God-all-knowing, all-powerful...

God waits... until everybody else... can't help you...

Long-suffering under grace... is long of mind... or long of soul...

Patience never quits... taking me through things... showing me who I

really am...

Maybe God is keeping me in long-suffering...

He's keeping me from things I could have...

But through long-suffering... I do not...

I'm in perfect peace...

What's good for you... can be bad for you... if it comes past your season...

Isolation... sometimes... is a gift..

Some things you need to go through... by yourself...

Persistence is key...

If I don't get anything else... I just want to get to the feet of Jesus...

humility...

I'm expecting... something... from God.

Section Five:

Dreams and Aspirations

Stand Up

Stand up for what you believe.

Don't stop—

because you can achieve.

Dream the hardest dream,

because it's yours.

Become the greatness

you strive for.

Don't take no for an answer

when it comes to your success.

The best is yet to come—

don't rest.

Respect your hustle.

Love your grind.

Build to be better.

The storms are coming—

but don't fret.

Life is a beast,

but you are its master.

And depending on how you treat it,

it will give back to you—

or take from you.

So it's important

that you stand up.

Light Is Powerful and Has Purpose

Light —

is power.

Light —

is purpose.

Our God is light.

Pure.

Precise.

Unstoppable.

Light reveals,

while darkness conceals.

Darkness moves fast,

but light moves with meaning.

This is a boxing match.

Power and knowledge

will always outlast speed.

Satan is out of his weight class.

His arms too short

to box with God.

It's All About You

It's about you —

learning to be happy.

But happiness —

it can spoil you

if you let it.

Joy lasts longer.

Joy sits deeper.

Joy is peace wearing patience.

Inside you

there's a war —

Heaven vs Hell,

life vs death,

peace vs chaos,

hope vs hopelessness.

It's a war called duality.

And duality —

lives in us all.

SuperStar

You know what?

I think I might be great.

Great at my craft —

great with my words —

great at telling stories with my hands.

On a pad, on a canvas, with paint under my nails —

I tell my past, my present, my maybe-future.

We can all grow. We can all love better.

It's about revolution.

It's about change.

It's about ART — damn it.

I won't stop.

I won't be silent.

I won't give up again.

I do this for me, not for your applause.

I am a Super Star.

Respect me like one.

You Wanna Know

You wanna know how I got over?

Over the hurt,

the pain,

the long nights that didn't end

until the morning cried?

I had to let go.

I had to do.

I had to see —

myself.

First spiritually,

then mentally,

then finally,

physically.

I had to do the work.

Stop thinking I was less,

and start believing I was more.

I was worth everything I deserved.

And once I knew that —

the people came.

The peace came.

The purpose came.

I had to let go of the past

and the entities that held me hostage.

That's how I got over.

Now let me help you.